MW00630439

TABLE *of* CONTENTS

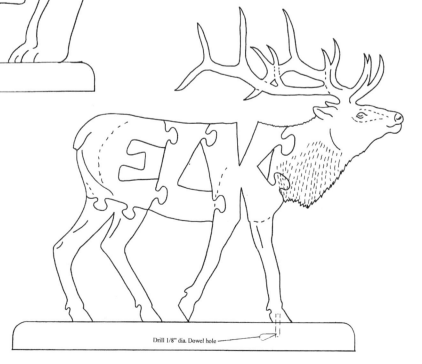

Drill 1/8" dia. Dowel hole

Introduction

*B*eginners and advanced scrollers alike will go wild for these classic animal projects. From a tiger stalking its prey to a mouse snacking on cheese, my booklet has something for everyone. Once you get the hang of it, you'll be turning these out in 20 minutes flat—so grab your bug spray and a favorite knapsack and follow me to the woods!

How to Use

*C*hoose a kind of wood; these patterns work best for fine-figured hardwoods such as walnut and maple. If you want the puzzle to be freestanding, choose wood with a thickness of ¾" (1.9cm) or more. Cut the wood to size and sand with 80-grit sandpaper, working up through the grits until you reach 220. Photocopy the pattern, cover the wood with blue painter's tape, and then attach the pattern to the wood with spray adhesive. Drill any blade-entry holes (for example, the center of the "A" in "Eagle") and cut the puzzles out on a scroll saw. For thicker blanks, I suggest at least a #5 reverse-tooth blade. The dotted lines are for paint reference only.

Remove the patterns and any excess sawdust. Then gently round over the sharp edges with 220- and then 320-grit sandpaper in a handheld sander. Finish as desired; I prefer a natural Danish oil, but you can add detail with thinned acrylics and then seal with matte spray lacquer or similar.

Note: If you're giving these puzzles to small children, consider omitting a few of the cut lines to make the pieces safe for play.

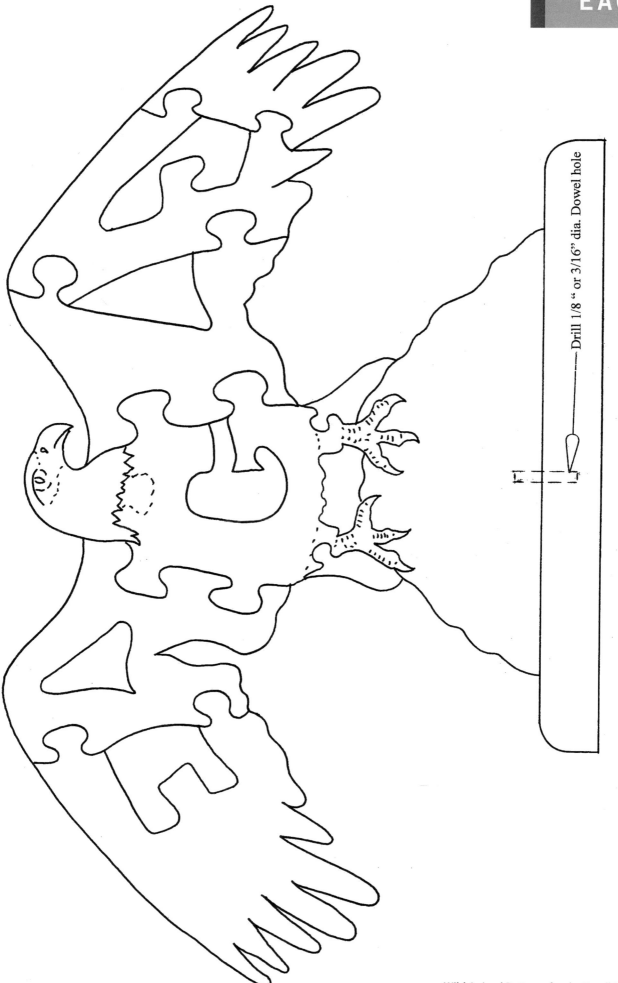

Drill 1/8 " or 3/16" dia. Dowel hole

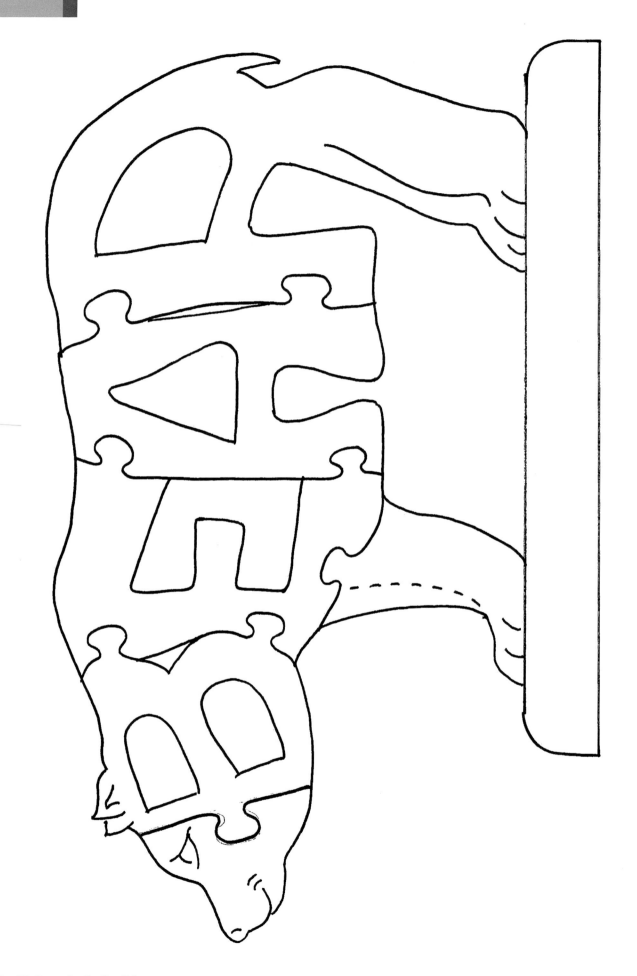

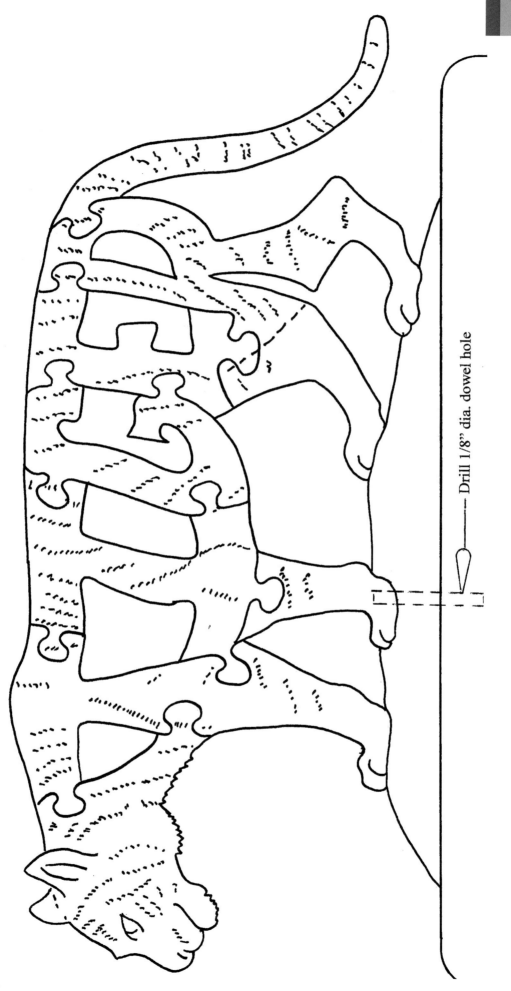

Drill 1/8" dia. dowel hole

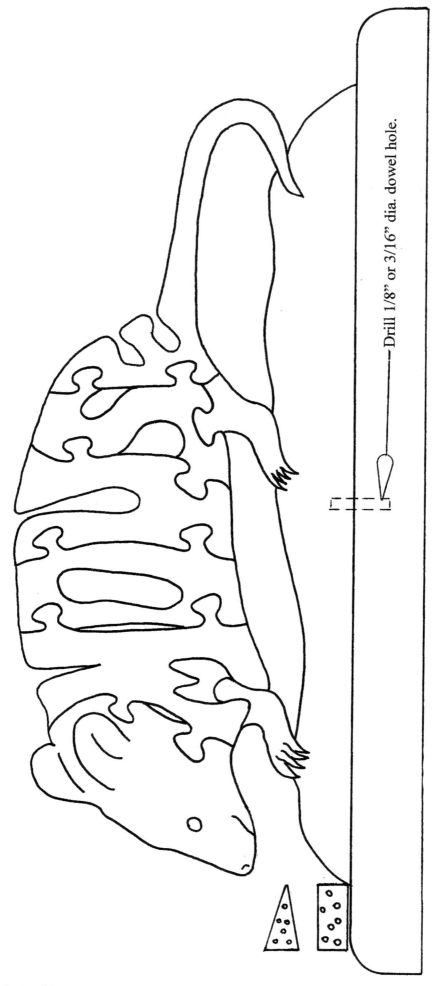

Drill 1/8" or 3/16" dia. dowel hole.

Drill 1/8 " or 3/16" dia. Dowel hole

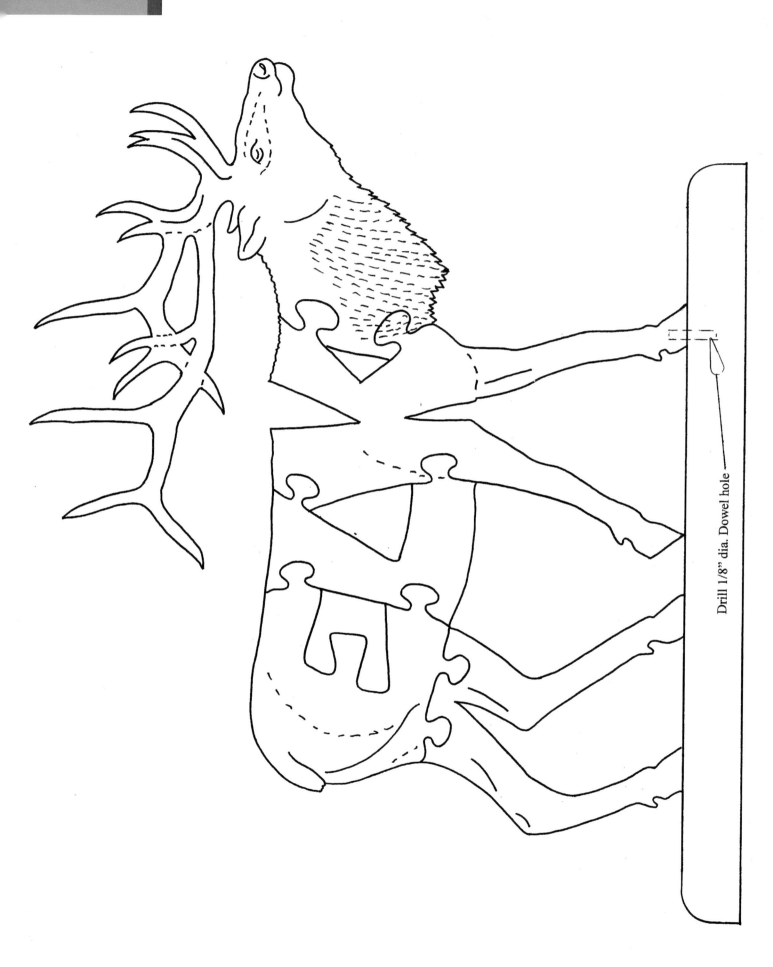

Drill 1/8" dia. Dowel hole

Get *Scroll Saw Woodworking & Crafts* Magazine
Delivered to Your Door 4 Times A Year!

Subscribe Today & Save 21%

SCROLL SAW WOODWORKING & CRAFTS

- Step-by-step, photo-illustrated instructions for all types of scrolling

- Dozens of full-size, removable, professionally drawn patterns

- Interesting and creative scroll saw artists, projects, and techniques

- Projects for all skill levels

- A wonderful resource for woodworkers at all levels

1-Year Cover Price ~~$31.96~~
Your Price $24.99
2-Year Cover Price ~~$63.92~~
Your Price $49.98
Canadian subscribers add $5.00. All other countries add $10.00 (U.S. funds only).

ORDER TODAY!

Visit www.FoxChapelPublishing.com or Call Toll-Free 1-800-457-9112

Classic Animal Projects for *Everyone*

From Jim Sweet, the inventor of Woodimals, comes this new collection of original puzzle patterns that are perfect for beginner to intermediate scroll sawyers! Featuring six full-size wild animal patterns, including a bear, tiger, elk, eagle, heron, and mouse, each completed and free-standing project uniquely spells the name of each animal – a Jim Sweet signature style. No matter your skill level, these projects are approachable for any scroll sawyer and can be completed in just 20 minutes!

Inside, you'll also find insightful how-to tips, from choosing which woods to use and transferring the patterns to sanding, finishing, and staining your projects. Great for gifting to the animal-lovers in your life or for proudly displaying as a cohesive collection, *Wild Animal Patterns* is the perfect resource to spark inspiration, further your skills, and try something completely new!

FOX CHAPEL
PUBLISHING

Wild Animal Patterns for the Scroll Saw

$7.99 US | $9.99 CAN | *£5.99 RRP UK*

ISBN: 978-1-4971-0118-0

9 781497 101180   50799

My Last Writes

The Ultimate End of Life Planning Workbook for Your Family

Plan for Your Family Before It's Too Late

Karen Wells